THESIS IN RESTORED YADAᶜ YAHUAH

Master of Biblical Restoration Studies

MBRS Book 5 —Master-Level Thesis in Yada Yahuah Restoration Mastery

The Official Student Textbook

DR. YERAL E. OGANDO

THESIS IN RESTORED YADAʿ YAHUAH

The Official Student Textbook for the Master of Biblical Restoration Studies (MBRS)

By

Dr. Yeral E. Ogando

Authored and published by
Dr. Yeral E. Ogando
Adopted for instructional use by
Yahuah Institute of Biblical Restoration, Inc.
As the core text for
The Master of Biblical Restoration Studies (MBRS) Program
Licensing Notice
This work is licensed to Yahuah Institute of Biblical Restoration, Inc. for instructional use pursuant to a separate licensing agreement. All rights not expressly granted are reserved by the author. No part of this work may be reproduced, distributed, or transmitted in any form or by any means without prior written permission of the author, except as permitted under the applicable licensing agreement.
© 2026 Dr. Yeral E. Ogando
All rights reserved.
No part of this publication may be reproduced, stored, or transmitted in any form or by any means—electronic, mechanical, photocopying, recording, or otherwise—without prior written permission of the publisher, except for brief quotations used in academic review.
Scripture quotations are taken exclusively from Dabar Yahuah Scriptures – www.yahuahbible.com.
This textbook is produced for academic, instructional, and theological training purposes within the MBRS program and affiliated courses.
"All instructional texts used by the MBRS Program are independently authored and published by Dr. Yeral E. Ogando. The Institute adopts these texts solely for instructional purposes and does not own, publish, or receive revenue from them."

ISBN: 978-1-946249-60-9

1. AUTHORIZATION & INSTITUTIONAL STATEMENT

This textbook, Foundations of Biblical Restoration, is authored and published by Dr. Yeral E. Ogando and is adopted and approved for instructional use by Yahuah Institute of Biblical Restoration, Inc. as the core instructional text for the Master of Biblical Restoration Studies (MBRS) program.

All doctrinal positions, terminology, instructional structures, and evaluative standards contained within this volume are governed exclusively by Dabar Yahuah Scriptures as preserved in the Scriptures recognized by the Institute: the inspired writings of the Tanakh (Old Testament), the preserved Apokryfos, and the Renewed Covenant (New Testament) writings.

This text operates within a closed canonical and theological framework for the academic cycle in which it is issued. No external denominational systems, philosophical methodologies, speculative Yada Yahuah (theology), or institutional traditions are permitted to govern interpretation, instruction, or assessment within the MBRS program.

This Student Edition is authorized for instructional use solely within the MBRS program.

Unauthorized reproduction, distribution, or use outside of Institute-approved instructional contexts is prohibited.

2. PREFACE & STATEMENT OF PURPOSE

Foundations of Biblical Restoration exists because Scripture itself demands restoration.

This textbook was not written to defend denominational systems, preserve inherited theology, or harmonize philosophical frameworks with Scripture. It was written to allow **Dabar Yahuah** to govern Yada Yahuah (theology) without competition.

Modern theology often begins with assumptions and searches Scripture for support. Restoration Yada Yahuah (theology) reverses that order. Scripture establishes authority, defines categories, diagnoses corruption, and reveals restoration according to divine intent rather than human tradition.

This book serves as the **single, integrated instructional text** for the Master of Biblical Restoration Studies (MBRS). It guides the student from Scriptural Witness through, *Yahuah: Restoration Guide,* the ***Origin of Evil:*** *Biblical Truths Hidden in Plain Sight,* the **Three Humanities**™: *The Division of Humanity in Yahuah's Plan* - Volume 1, and th*e* **Three Humanities**™: *The Restoration of the First Humanity in Yahuah's Plan*—culminating in independent thesis defense.

3. STATEMENT OF PURPOSE

The purpose of this textbook is to:

    Establish Scripture as the sole governing authority

    Restore biblical categories obscured by tradition and translation

    Define evil without attributing corruption to Yahuah

    Explain humanity through the **Three Humanities**™ framework

    Present restoration as transformation, not repair

    Prepare students to defend **Restoration Yada Yahuah** (theology)

independently and accurately

This text is not devotional. It is not speculative. It is instructional, corrective, and authoritative.

4. PROGRAM LEARNING OUTCOMES
MASTER OF BIBLICAL RESTORATION STUDIES (MBRS)

Upon successful completion of the MBRS program, the student will be able to:

1. Demonstrate Covenantal Reasoning across the full body of Scripture, integrating the Tanakh (Old Testament), Apokryfos, and Renewed Covenant (New Testament) writings without contradiction.

2. Explain Scriptural authority as divinely originated, canonically bounded, and covenantal preserved.

3. Define evil, corruption, judgment, and restoration using Scriptural categories alone, without reliance on philosophical or denominational frameworks.

4. Articulate the Three Humanities™ framework (First, Second, Third Humanities and the Variant) using Scripture-governed anthropology and lineage Yada Yahuah (theology).

5. Distinguish between sin, corruption, and Creational alteration, explaining why restoration requires transformation rather than moral repair.

6. Apply covenant language discipline responsibly, demonstrating how words govern doctrine and prevent theological distortion.

7. Defend Restoration Yada Yahuah (theology) from creation to consummation as a unified, Scripture-consistent system.

8. Produce and defend a master-level thesis grounded exclusively in Scripture, demonstrating doctrinal clarity, canonical consistency, and methodological integrity.

5. HOW TO USE THIS TEXTBOOK

This textbook is designed for **structured, sequential use** within the MBRS program.

STUDENT RESPONSIBILITIES

- Read all assigned Scripture before engaging commentary or explanations.
- Follow the progression of weeks and months without skipping sections.
- Use only Institute-approved Scriptural sources when completing assignments.
- Adhere strictly to locked templates, prompts, and evaluation criteria.

- Demonstrate mastery through clarity, Scripture use, and disciplined reasoning.

INSTRUCTIONAL STRUCTURE

- Each Term builds upon previous authority and doctrine.
- Each Month introduces defined instructional goals.
- Each Week focuses on specific Scriptural concepts.
- Assessments measure integration and reasoning, not memorization.

This text is not designed for casual reading.
It is designed for **formation, correction, and qualification.**

Students who attempt to bypass structure, introduce external systems, or rely on speculation will not advance.

6. ACADEMIC & SCRIPTURAL INTEGRITY STATEMENT

Enrollment in the MBRS program constitutes agreement to the following standards:

- **Scripture governs all conclusions.**
- **Dabar Yahuah is the highest authority.**
- No denominational, philosophical, or speculative systems may override Scripture.
- All work must be original, truthful, and accurately cited.
- Plagiarism, doctrinal innovation, or misrepresentation of Scripture results in disqualification.
- Advancement is evaluative, not automatic.

This program values **clarity over creativity, submission over speculation, and truth over tradition.**

The goal is not affirmation, but formation.

Authorized Textual Resources and Access

The instructional texts and Scriptural resources referenced within the Master of Biblical Restoration Studies (MBRS) program are made available through designated platforms.

Primary reference texts and supporting source materials authored by Dr. Yeral E. Ogando are openly accessible at www.yahuahdabar.com. These materials may be read online by any visitor. Registration allows users to download PDF versions of the source texts. These materials are publicly available and are not restricted to enrolled students.

The Dabar Yahuah Scriptures, including the Tanakh (Old Testament), Apokryfos, and Renewed Covenant (New Testament) writings, are openly accessible for online reading at www.yahuahbible.com. These texts are provided as the authorized Scriptural reference for the MBRS program and are available to all readers.

For Scriptural study and term-level consultation, students are instructed to use the Dabar Yahuah Scriptures App, including its Strong Concordance tools for Hebrew and Greek reference. This tool is used for confirming word forms, meanings, and Scriptural usage in alignment with the Institute's instructional framework.

The Student Edition textbooks, however, are not publicly distributed through these websites. Student textbooks are provided through the Institute's instructional platform or authorized course distribution channels, with the exception of the Amazon print edition.

These access distinctions are intentional and form part of the Institute's instructional and evaluative framework.

Contents

TERM V · MONTH 1 10

TERM V – MONTH 1 - WEEK 65 12

TERM V – MONTH 1 - WEEK 66 — CORRUPTION RECOGNITION 12

TERM V – MONTH 1 - WEEK 67 — RESTORATION RECOGNITION 13

TERM V – MONTH 1 - WEEK 68 — SYSTEM INTEGRITY 14

WEEK 69 — CANONICAL MATRIX 18

WEEK 70 — COVENANT LANGUAGE RESEARCH FILE 18

WEEK 71 — CHAPTER 1 DRAFT 19

WEEK 72 — CHAPTER 2 DRAFT 19

TERM V · MONTH 3—FULL MANUSCRIPT DEVELOPMENT &
ARGUMENT COMPLETION 21

WEEK 73 — CHAPTER 3 DRAFT 22

WEEK 74 — REMAINING CHAPTERS 22

WEEK 75 — FULL MANUSCRIPT ASSEMBLY 22

WEEK 76 - FORMAL SUBMISSION — MONTH 3 22

TERM V · MONTH 4 — QUALIFICATION, INTEGRITY & FINAL DECISION 24

WEEK 77 — FINAL MANUSCRIPT PREPARATION 25

WEEK 78 — DOCTRINAL INTEGRITY RESOLUTION 25

WEEK 79 — PUBLICATION READINESS PACKET 25

WEEK 80 - FORMAL SUBMISSION — MONTH 4 25

FINAL DECISION — MONTH— THESIS OUTCOME, PUBLICATION
PATHWAY & AUTHORSHIP INTENT 26

CONGRATULATORY & ACADEMIC ACKNOWLEDGMENT 28

THE DOCTORAL FORMATION PATHWAY 29

REQUIRED DOCTORAL FORMATION STAGES 30

DOCTORAL CANDIDACY & ORIGINAL CONTRIBUTION 30

FINAL PROGRAM DECLARATION 31

FINAL MBRS PROGRAM CONCLUSION 32

TERM V · MONTH 1
THE FUNCTION OF TERM V

TERM V exists for one purpose:
to determine whether Yada Yahuah has fully transferred.
This term does not add material.
It does not expand the system.
It does not refine doctrine.

It tests whether the student can:
- interpret Scripture without guidance
- apply the Humanity Equations without prompts
- preserve causal direction without correction
- defend restoration logic without collapsing categories
- articulate the entire Plan of Yahuah as one unified system

TERM V STRUCTURE

Month 1 — Deductive Demonstration (Qualification Phase)
The student is no longer instructed.
They are shown the framework in operation and required to deduce, not repeat.
The question governing Month 1 is singular:
Has Restoration Yada Yahuah become native to the student's reasoning?
If yes — mastery is demonstrated.
If not — the framework has not yet transferred.
This month functions as a diagnostic threshold, not a teaching block.

Months 2–4 — Thesis (Independent Synthesis Phase)
Instruction ends.
Supervision remains.

The student must independently:
- construct a full-system articulation of Yahuah's Plan
- defend separation, judgment, and inheritance
- trace the Three Humanities from origin to consummation
- demonstrate internal coherence across all terms

No new guidance is given.
No scaffolding is provided.
No corrective instruction is offered.
What the student produces reflects what now lives within them.

THE DEDUCTIVE EXPERIMENT
From Reception to Recognition

MONTH PURPOSE
Term V · Month 1 exists to determine whether the student now operates from Yada' Yahuah rather than learning about it.

This month does not:
- introduce new material
- explain prior material
- guide interpretation

It presents revealed structures only and observes whether the student can deduce truth without assistance.

This month is the gateway to the Thesis.

MONTH 1 STRUCTURE OVERVIEW
- Week 65 — Recognition of Creational Order
- Week 66 — Recognition of Corruption Logic
- Week 67 — Recognition of Restoration Logic
- Week 68 — System Integrity & Boundary Defense

Each week:
- uses already-given material only
- contains no teaching explanations
- requires deductive outputs
- escalates in boundary pressure

TERM V – MONTH 1 - WEEK 65 — CREATIONAL RECOGNITION

Identifying What Yahuah Authored

Governing Material

- **Humanity Equation: Y + A = FH**

Text Focus: The First Humanity (FH)

- Scripture Set:
  - Bereshith 1–2
  - Bereshith 5:1–3
  - Iyov 33:4

Deductive Task

- Without redefining terms, the student must demonstrate:
- Why the First Humanity is the only lawful baseline
- Why Ruach transmission must be paternal
- Why creation completeness precedes human action
- Why identity precedes obedience

Disallowed Moves

- Moral framing of the Fall
- Evolutionary language
- Treating FH as symbolic or abstract

Pass Signal

The student reasons from origin, not behavior.

TERM V – MONTH 1 - WEEK 66 — CORRUPTION RECOGNITION

Identifying What Yahuah Did NOT Author

Governing Material

Humanity Equations:

- AW + HW = N
- NM + PW = N

- PM + NW = MH
- ***Text Focus:***
  - The Second Humanity
  - The Third Humanity (Mixed Humanity)

Scripture Set
- Bereshith 6
- Bemidbar 13:32–33
- Devarim 9:1–2

Deductive Task

The student must:
- Explain why corruption is genealogical, not moral
- Demonstrate why Nephilim lineage is irredeemable
- Distinguish clearly between:
  - Nephilim
  - Mixed Humanity
- Prove why separation is protective logic

Disallowed Moves
- Treating giants as metaphors
- Attributing corruption to environment alone
- Moralizing Nephilim judgment

Pass Signal

The student preserves inheritance asymmetry without collapsing categories.

TERM V – MONTH 1 - WEEK 67 — RESTORATION RECOGNITION

Identifying What Yahuah Alone Can Restore

Governing Material
- Humanity Restoration Equation:
  - $Y \oplus HW = Y$
- Text Focus:

- The Variant (Yahusha Ha'Mashiyach)

Scripture Set
- Yochanan 1:14
- Mattithyahu 1:18–25
- Yochanan 20:22

Deductive Task

The student must:
- Prove why the Variant is singular
- Explain why Yahusha is not inheritable
- Demonstrate how all inheritance laws are bypassed
- Preserve the distinction between:
  - Restoration
  - Reproduction

Disallowed Moves
- Treating Yahusha as a template humanity
- Introducing Fourth Humanity logic
- Geneticizing salvation

Pass Signal

The student protects Yahusha's uniqueness without weakening restoration.

TERM V – MONTH 1 - WEEK 68 — SYSTEM INTEGRITY

Defending the Completed Framework

Governing Material
- Final Humanity Equation:
  - $Y + RT = FH$
- Integrated Use:
  - All prior equations
  - All prior definitions

Scripture Set
- 1 Korínthios 15
- Rómĕos 8

- Apokálypsis 21–22

Deductive Task

The student must:
- Trace the full arc:
  - Creation → Corruption → Restoration → Completion
- Prove why restoration returns humanity to FH
- Demonstrate why corruption cannot re-emerge
- Defend inheritance as nature, not reward

Disallowed Moves
- Probationary eternity
- Cyclical rebellion
- Symbolic-only fulfillment

Pass Signal

The system remains closed, stable, and irreversible.

MONTH 1 FINAL EVALUATION (NO ESSAY)

Required Submission
- One structured system articulation (format free)

Must show:
- Boundary preservation
- Correct deduction
- No speculation
- No emotional framing

Evaluation Outcome
- Qualified → Student advances to Thesis (Term V · Months 2–4)
- Not Qualified → Remediation required before Thesis eligibility

FINAL STATEMENT – MONTH 1

This month proves whether the student:
- knows about Yahuah

or
- knows Yahuah as He has revealed Himself

Yada' Yahuah does not argue.

It recognizes.

Instruction ends here.

Only demonstration remains.

TERM V · MONTHS 2-4
FINAL THESIS PHASE
Construction · Verification · Qualification

TERM V · MONTH 2
ARGUMENT CONSTRUCTION & EARLY CHAPTER DEVELOPMENT

MONTH 2 CONTEXT
Term V · Month 2 marks the transition from approved framework to active thesis construction.
The student is no longer proposing ideas. The thesis is now being written, tested, and structurally proven.

This month determines whether the thesis:
- can sustain canonical argumentation
- maintains covenant language discipline
- functions beyond conceptual design

Failure at this stage prevents larger failure later.

Month 2 Purpose
By the end of Month 2, the student must demonstrate:
- a complete canonical research framework
- controlled and defensible covenant language foundations
- two fully drafted chapters
- confirmation that the thesis is viable at book length

This month proves the thesis can be written, not merely imagined.

Non-Negotiable Standards — Month 2
- Scripture governs argumentation
- Dabar Yahuah Scriptures remain the sole authority
- Covenant language discipline is mandatory
- Cross-canonical consistency is required

- No speculative expansion beyond approved scope
- No deviation from the approved blueprint

Unauthorized deviation halts progression.

Submission Structure Clarification — Month 2

The developmental elements outlined below function as internal student-governed requirements, not individual submissions.

Only one formal submission is required for Term V · Month 2, due at the end of the month.

That submission must demonstrate full and complete execution of all internal development requirements listed below as a unified packet.

INTERNAL DEVELOPMENT SEQUENCE — MONTH 2

WEEK 69 — CANONICAL MATRIX

Purpose

To demonstrate that the thesis is anchored across the full Scriptural corpus, not dependent on isolated texts.

Required Development

- 8–12 core doctrinal terms
- Old Covenant anchors
- Apokryfos anchors
- Renewed Covenant anchors
- Explanation of how each corpus contributes to doctrine

WEEK 70 — COVENANT LANGUAGE RESEARCH FILE

Purpose

To establish linguistic control before doctrinal expansion.

Required Development

- 3–5 key thesis terms
- Original-language roots

- Scriptural usage across contexts
- Doctrinal implications
- Explicit semantic limits

WEEK 71 — CHAPTER 1 DRAFT

Purpose

To establish thesis tone, authority, and structural discipline.

Required Development

- Full Chapter 1 draft
- Clear thesis alignment
- Structured argumentation
- Scripture governing all major claims

WEEK 72 — CHAPTER 2 DRAFT

Purpose

To demonstrate argument continuity and sustainability.

Required Development

- Full Chapter 2 draft
- Logical development from Chapter 1
- No redundancy or contradiction

FORMAL SUBMISSION — MONTH 2

Submission Title

Month 2 Thesis Development Packet

Required Contents

- Canonical Matrix
- Covenant Language Research File
- Chapter 1 Draft
- Chapter 2 Draft

MONTH 2 COMPLETION RULE

Advancement requires supervisor-issued status:

"ON TRACK — PROCEED TO MONTH 3."

Structural failure or doctrinal instability must be corrected before advancement.

MONTH 2 CLOSING STATEMENT

"A thesis proves itself not by ideas alone, but by sustained, disciplined argument."

TERM V· MONTH 3—FULL MANUSCRIPT DEVELOPMENT & ARGUMENT COMPLETION

Month 3 Context
Month 3 is the execution phase.
All planning is complete. All foundations are verified.
This month determines whether the student can:
- complete a book-length argument
- maintain consistency across chapters
- finish without doctrinal collapse

Month 3 Purpose
By the end of Month 3, the student must have:
- all chapters fully drafted
- a complete manuscript following the approved blueprint
- supervisor review and written feedback
- a defined revision pathway

Completion is mandatory. Polishing comes later.

Non-Negotiable Standards — Month 3
- Strict adherence to approved blueprint
- No new doctrinal claims
- No scope expansion
- Scripture governs all arguments
- Covenant language discipline maintained
- Structural coherence across chapters

Submission Structure Clarification — Month 3
The elements outlined below function as internal development milestones, not individual submissions.
Only one formal submission is required for Term V · Month 3, due at the end of the month.
That submission must present the entire manuscript as a unified work.

INTERNAL DEVELOPMENT SEQUENCE — MONTH 3

WEEK 73 — CHAPTER 3 DRAFT

Purpose

To demonstrate argument sustainability beyond opening chapters.

Required Development

- Full Chapter 3 draft
- Exact blueprint compliance
- No new themes or claims

WEEK 74 — REMAINING CHAPTERS

Purpose

To complete all remaining chapters required for thesis resolution.

Required Development

- Chapter 4 draft
- Any additional chapters
- Full blueprint alignment

WEEK 75 — FULL MANUSCRIPT ASSEMBLY

Purpose

To consolidate the thesis into a unified document.

Required Development

- Title page
- Abstract
- All chapters
- Preliminary conclusion
- Scripture citations

WEEK 76 - FORMAL SUBMISSION — MONTH 3

Submission Title

Complete Draft Manuscript

Required Contents
- Full manuscript
- All chapters in blueprint order
- Preliminary conclusion
- Proper Scripture citations

Month 3 Completion Rule

Advancement requires supervisor-issued status:

"Draft Accepted for Qualification."

Failure to submit a complete manuscript results in delay.

MONTH 3 CLOSING STATEMENT

"A thesis is not complete when it sounds convincing, but when it stands coherent from first word to last."

TERM V · MONTH 4 — QUALIFICATION, INTEGRITY & FINAL DECISION

MONTH 4 CONTEXT

Month 4 is the final authority phase.

No research. No expansion. No revision beyond correction.

This month determines:

- doctrinal integrity
- teaching suitability
- degree conferral

Month 4 Purpose

By the end of Month 4, the student must have:

- a finalized manuscript
- demonstrated doctrinal coherence
- prepared the work for publication or teaching
- received final program outcome

Non-Negotiable Standards — Month 4

- Fidelity to approved scope
- No new doctrinal claims
- No new covenant language work
- Canonical consistency throughout
- All supervisor feedback resolved

Submission Structure Clarification — Month 4

The qualification elements outlined below function as internal resolution requirements.

Only one formal submission is required for Term V · Month 4, due at the end of the month.

This submission represents the authoritative final thesis package.

INTERNAL QUALIFICATION SEQUENCE — MONTH 4

WEEK 77 — FINAL MANUSCRIPT PREPARATION

Purpose

To finalize the authoritative version of the thesis.

WEEK 78 — DOCTRINAL INTEGRITY RESOLUTION

Required Categories

- Canon
- Corruption
- Divided Humanity
- Restoration
- Fulfillment

WEEK 79 — PUBLICATION READINESS PACKET

Required Contents

- Back-cover summary
- Final table of contents
- Audience and use statement
- Teaching-use summary (if applicable)

WEEK 80 - FORMAL SUBMISSION — MONTH 4

Submission Title

Final Thesis & Qualification Packet

Required Contents

- Final manuscript
- Doctrinal integrity fully resolved
- Publication readiness materials

FINAL DECISION — MONTH— THESIS OUTCOME, PUBLICATION PATHWAY & AUTHORSHIP INTENT

Nature of the Thesis Work

The thesis produced in Term V is not conceived merely as an academic exercise. It is designed, evaluated, and refined as a book-caliber work suitable for publication, teaching, and long-term instructional use.

Where the work meets the highest standards of clarity, doctrinal integrity, and transferability, the Institute views the thesis not only as a qualification artifact, but as a potential future textbook and reference work within the Restoration Yada Yahuah curriculum.

Publication Intent

When a thesis is deemed publication-ready:

- The Institute may assist the student (author) in preparing the work for publication
- The work may be used as an instructional text within the Institute (where applicable)
- The student retains full authorship and primary publishing rights

Publication support does not alter authorship.

The thesis remains the intellectual work of the student.

Author Rights & Royalties

When the thesis is published in its original language:

- The student is recognized as the sole author
- All standard publication royalties belong to the student

Translated Editions & Shared Royalty Structure

If the Institute undertakes translation of the work into additional languages:

- The Institute retains eighty percent (80%) of royalties associated with translated editions
- The student-author receives twenty percent (20%) of royalties associated

with translated editions
- Original-language editions remain the exclusive property of the student-author.
- This royalty structure reflects the Institute's responsibility for translation, Yada Yahuah review, editorial oversight, formatting, and distribution, while preserving ongoing author participation.
- These provisions are governed by existing thesis and student agreements and are reiterated here for clarity of intent, not renegotiation.

Outcome Determination

At the conclusion of Term V · Month 4, one of the following outcomes is issued:
- Approved
- Approved with Minor Revisions
- Revision Required
- Not Approved

Only Approved or Approved with Minor Revisions result in:
- graduation from the program
- eligibility for authorship recognition
- eligibility for publication consideration

A thesis may qualify for graduation without being selected for publication. Publication is an opportunity, not an entitlement.

Institutional Vision

The Institute does not seek merely to graduate students.
It seeks to form articulate, disciplined, and faithful stewards of truth whose work can serve others beyond the classroom.
Where a thesis achieves sufficient clarity, coherence, and doctrinal stability, it may become part of the living instructional body of the Institute.

Final Program Statement

"A thesis is complete when truth is articulated clearly, defended faithfully, and ready to serve others without confusion."

CONGRATULATORY & ACADEMIC ACKNOWLEDGMENT

Congratulations.

You have completed a course of study that requires more than intellectual engagement.

You have submitted to:
- Scriptural authority over tradition
- Discipline over speculation
- Structure over opinion
  Restoration over compromise

Few complete such a program because few are willing to be corrected at the level of foundations.

By completing this work, you are no longer a consumer of Yada' Yahuah frameworks.

You are now qualified to interpret, articulate, and defend Restoration Yada' Yahuah within the boundaries established by Scripture and preserved by disciplined method.

This qualification carries responsibility.

STATEMENT OF DEGREE CONFERRAL

Upon approval of the Final Thesis and satisfaction of all academic and doctrinal requirements, the student is eligible for the conferral of the non-accredited ecclesiastical degree:

Master of Biblical Restoration Studies (MBRS)

This degree affirms demonstrated competence in:
- Covenantal Reasoning
- Covenant language discipline
- System-level Yada' Yahuah coherence
- Academic and doctrinal integrity

Degree conferral does not grant autonomous doctrinal authority.

It confirms readiness for advanced responsibility under Scripture.

THE MBRS AS FOUNDATION — NOT TERMINUS

This degree does not represent the completion of learning.

It represents the restoration of foundations.

The Master of Biblical Restoration Studies establishes the minimum Yada' Yahuah architecture required for advanced formation. It ensures that any further **work is built on:**

- a restored canon,
- correct doctrinal categories,
- covenantal logic,
- and disciplined method.

The Master restores what must be restored before original contribution is permitted.

Doctoral work does not repair foundations.

Doctoral work refines, extends, and contributes from them.

No student is considered finished at this stage.

They are considered properly grounded.

THE DOCTORAL FORMATION PATHWAY

From Restored Foundations to Original Contribution

Graduates who demonstrate readiness may be considered for entry into the Doctoral Formation Pathway in Restored Yada' Yahuah.

The doctoral degree is not entered directly.

It is reached only through a multi-stage, cumulative formation process designed to produce full-canon scholars capable of original contribution without doctrinal fragmentation.

The MBRS is the gateway — not the doctorate.

Nature of Doctoral Formation

Doctoral formation is not a single degree level.

It is an ordered sequence of required stages, each governing a core corpus of Scripture.

- No certificates are issued.

- No stages may be skipped.
- Progress is recorded under Institute authority.

This structure exists to eliminate partial Yadaʿ Yahuah, fragmented doctrine, and speculative systems.

REQUIRED DOCTORAL FORMATION STAGES

- Stage I — Pentateuch Formation
  Mastery of creation order, covenant foundations, humanity, and law
  No doctoral work proceeds without Pentateuchal mastery.
- Stage II — Historical & Prophetic Formation
  Integration of Yasharal's history as covenant testimony and prophecy as covenant lawsuit.
- Stage III — Apocryphal & Second Temple Formation
  Resolution of corruption origins, Watchers, hybridization, and canonical continuity gaps.
- Stage IV — Gospels & Apostolic Formation
  Confirmation of Messiah-centered fulfillment and covenant continuity.
- Stage V — The Teachings of Yahusha Ha Mashiyach
  Synthesis of all prior stages into a unified, Messiah-centered Restoration framework.

Completion of this stage grants eligibility for doctoral candidacy.

DOCTORAL CANDIDACY & ORIGINAL CONTRIBUTION

Completion of the Doctor Pathway formation stages does not confer a doctoral degree or credential.

These stages provide foundational preparation only.

After all formation requirements are completed, a student may be approved to enter the Final Doctorate Program as a doctoral candidate in Restored Yadaʿ Yahuah.

Doctoral candidacy is not a degree and carries no academic title.

It is formal authorization to begin doctoral-level original contribution.

Candidacy permits:
- original research
- participation in doctoral seminar
- proposal of a doctoral capstone work

The doctoral capstone must present original contribution, not repetition, in one **of the following forms:**
- a Doctoral Dissertation in Restored Yada' Yahuah, or
- a Doctoral Teaching Corpus in Canonical Restoration.

The doctoral degree is awarded only after successful completion and approval of the Final Doctorate Program.

FINAL PROGRAM DECLARATION

The goal of this program was never information.
It was restoration.

Restoration of:
- Scriptural authority
- Doctrinal boundaries
- Yada' Yahuah clarity
- Covenantal alignment
- The Master restores foundations.

Doctoral formation refines and contributes.
Eternity judges faithfulness.
May those who complete this work continue forward with humility, discipline, and obedience — remembering always:
Restoration does not end with understanding.
It continues with responsibility.

FINAL MBRS PROGRAM CONCLUSION

From Instruction to Stewardship — The Completion of the Master of Biblical Restoration Studies

The Master of Biblical Restoration Studies has now completed its work. Across five progressive stages, foundations were restored, authority was reordered, corruption was identified, humanity was mapped, restoration was disclosed, and covenant structure was stabilized. The student has passed from reception to formation, from formation to mastery, and from mastery to demonstration.

No further instruction remains within this program.
The architecture has been delivered in full.
MBRS Book 5 has not added doctrine, theory, or system. Instead, it has required the student to prove that Yadaʿ Yahuah has transferred from external framework to internal reasoning. The thesis phase has tested whether the student can preserve boundaries without supervision, defend covenant logic without collapse, and articulate restoration without distortion.
At this point, the student ceases to be a recipient of structured teaching.

They become a steward of restored knowledge.
The Master of Biblical Restoration Studies therefore concludes not with information, but with responsibility. What has been restored must now be guarded. What has been clarified must now be preserved. What has been demonstrated must now be lived, taught, and defended within the limits of Scripture and under the authority of Yahuah alone.
Instruction has ended.
Stewardship begins.
May those who complete this path walk forward in humility, restraint, and faithfulness — remembering always:
Restoration does not end with understanding.
It continues with responsibility.

www.ingramcontent.com/pod-product-compliance
Lightning Source LLC
Chambersburg PA
CBHW081509040426
42446CB00017B/3446